Copyright 2024 Shari Harpaz

All Rights Reserved. No part of this publication may be reproduced, distributed, or transmitted in any form or by any means, including photoshopping, recording, or other electronic or mechanical methods without prior written permission of the author and publisher, except in the case of the brief quotations embodied in reviews and certain other noncommercial uses permitted by copyright law. For information regarding permission, email the author at shbooksllc@gmail.com

This book is a work of fiction. Names, characters, and incidents, are either the product of the author's imagination or are used fictitiously, and any resemblance to actual persons living or dead, business establishment, events, or locales, is entirely coincidental.

First Edition Book, 2023

978-1-957506-76-0 – paperback
978-1-957506-77-7 – hardback

Published by Skinny Brown Dog Media Atlanta, GA
www.skinnybrowndogmedia.com
Distributed by Skinny Brown Dog Media

Dedication

Casey: Always lead with compassion and surround yourself with people that bring out the best in you. You are the prize.

Dana & Jack: You make your Titi proud each and every day. Never stop chasing your dreams. Love you more.

Molly was bursting with excitement. She was going to her best friend Julia's house for her first sleepover, and she couldn't wait to get there.

"Mommy, Mommy, can we please go right this very second?" Molly squealed as she bounced into the living room, her overnight bag falling off her shoulder.

"PJs, toothbrush, bunny. Looks like you have everything," her mom said as she checked what Molly had packed. "I can't wait. Come on Mom. Let's go!"

Molly picked up her dog Rosy. "Make sure you snuggle Mommy while I'm gone, okay?"

Julia was eagerly waiting on the front steps with her grandma and younger brother, Henry. Her grandma lived with them and was in charge this weekend.

"Hi Ms. Kim," Molly smiled as she quickly gave her mom a big hug, then raced inside with Julia. "Thank you for having Molly over," Molly's mom said. "She is always welcome in our home," replied Julia's grandma, as Henry squirmed in her arms.

SHE LEAVES A LITTLE
sparkle
WHEREVER SHE GOES

Molly and Julia were playing with the dollhouse when Julia's grandma summoned them. "Girls, come down to the kitchen. I have a surprise for you."

"Hurray," they squealed when they saw the decorate-your-own treats! "Thank you, Hammi" Julia hugged her grandma, before she joined Molly, who had already started sampling the goodies.

"Julia, what is this?" Molly asked, pointing to a bowl. "That's ddalgi bingsu. It's strawberry shaved ice, my favorite Korean dessert," Julia proudly replied.

The girls chatted as they dipped marshmallows in chocolate and added toppings to the cookies. "This is such a fun sleepover so far," Molly mumbled with her mouth full of sprinkles.

Henry, and his high-chair, were covered with squished strawberries and chocolate.

Stuffed with treats, the girls went to play school. "Class, today we're going on a field trip to the aquarium," Molly said using her teacher voice. Julia shouted out, "Will we see any sharks? I'm scared of sharks. Can we feed the stingrays?"

Just then the doorbell rang unexpectedly. "Hooray, Emma's here," Julia cheered as she jumped to her feet.

Molly stood frozen at the top of the stairs. What is happening? Julia never said someone else was coming to our sleepover. This is the worst thing ever, Molly grumbled.

She was lost in thought when Emma cheerfully waved. "Hi Molly, I'm so excited to be here." Molly quietly mumbled, "Oh hi Emma. I didn't know you were coming."

"Molly. Emma. Let's go outside. Last one to the swings is a rotten egg," Julia giggled as she raced out back. Emma skipped behind her, but Molly just stared at the floor.

"Molly, what are you waiting for?" Julia shouted as she pumped her legs higher and higher. Molly didn't really feel like playing now that Emma had joined, but Julia's new swingset was hard to resist.

Emma showed off some tricks on the monkey bars that she had learned in gymnastics. "Wow Emma, you're really good," Molly cheered as she waited for her own turn.

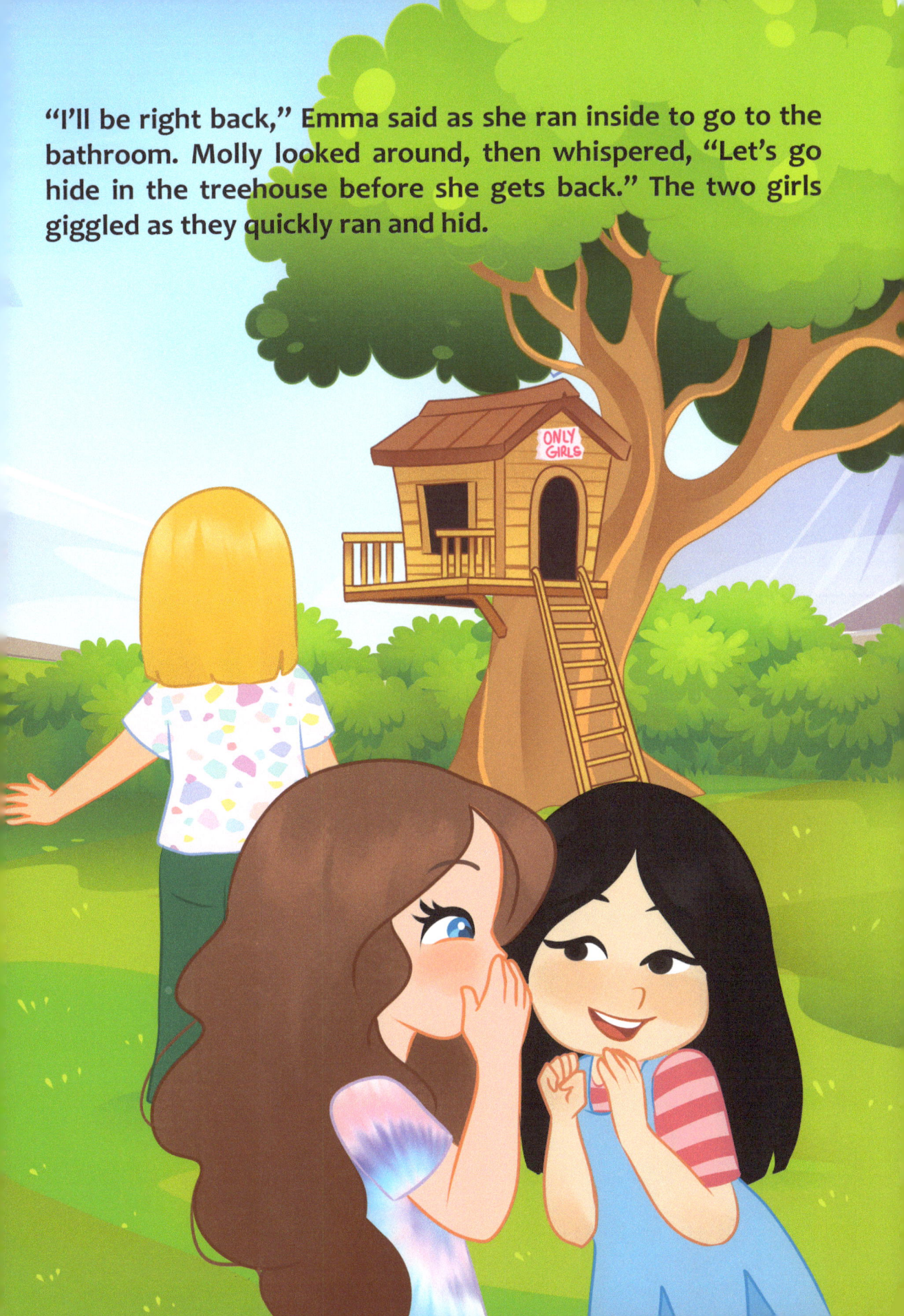

"I'll be right back," Emma said as she ran inside to go to the bathroom. Molly looked around, then whispered, "Let's go hide in the treehouse before she gets back." The two girls giggled as they quickly ran and hid.

Emma came back outside, but couldn't find her friends. "Julia? Molly? Where are you?"

"Come out, come out wherever you are?"

Inside the treehouse, Molly and Julia could hear Emma calling their names. Julia smiled and whispered, "Molly, let's poke our heads out the window and shout 'Boo'."

Julia tried to stand up, but Molly gently pulled her arm and shook her head 'no'. She was happy to have Julia all to herself again. "Not yet," whispered Molly.

Suddenly, they realized Emma had stopped calling their names. They looked out and saw Emma sitting on the grass, wiping tears away. Molly's heart sank; what started off as a fun idea had gone all wrong.

Molly and Julia scurried down the treehouse stairs shouting, "Emma, Emma we're right here." Emma was picking at the grass. "Why did you hide from me? That was really mean. If you don't want me here, I'll just leave," she stated.

"I'm really sorry Emma" Julia said as she tried giving her a hug. But Emma kept her arms crossed. "We didn't mean to… we thought we were…. I'm really sorry, Emma," Molly tried to explain.

The apologies were nice, but they didn't seem to help. "What do we do, Molly?" Julia shrugged, feeling badly for what they had done.

"Oh I have an idea, Julia. Wait here Emma. I think we can fix this. We'll be right back." Molly took Julia's hand and ran towards the house.

"Girls, is everything ok?" Hammi asked as Molly and Julia ran past. Hammi noticed Emma was left sitting alone. "Emma, do you want to tell me what happened?"

Emma was in the middle of explaining, when Molly and Julia returned waving something in the air. "Emma, we didn't mean to hurt your feelings," they said as they handed her butterfly-shaped notes.

Emma's smile grew as she read the special notes. "Thank you for these. You know how much I love butterflies."

"Group hug," the friends shouted all at the same time! Hammi proudly watched. "Okay girls, it's time for dinner and movie night." The girls jumped up and down, still hugging.

"First one in pajamas gets to pick the movie," Hammi announced as the friends scurried to get changed.

The living room was set up for their picnic dinner with chicken fingers, veggies and dumplings. "Hammi, these dumplings are delicious," Molly said as she filled her plate.

After their delicious dessert of Bingsu and loaded cookies, the girls climbed into their sleeping bags. They had chosen to watch *Mia Makes A Movie*, even though they had seen it 1,000 times!

"Good night. Hope you dream about dancing puppies again, Molly," Julia yawned. Their giggles faded as they drifted off to sleep.

The next morning, Molly hugged Julia and Emma goodbye. "Thank you. This was the best sleepover ever. I can't wait for the next one."

"How was your first sleepover?" Mom asked as they drove away. "It was great! We made our own desserts and played with dolls and…" Molly paused.

"Well actually Mom, I kind of did something that wasn't very nice." Her mom nodded, waiting to hear what happened. "I was surprised and mad that Emma showed up. When we were playing outside, I told Julia we should hide from her. And then Emma cried."

"We said we were sorry, but it didn't help. I told Julia we should make her sorry notes. She loved it. We had the best time together after that." Her mom smiled warmly, "I'm proud of you and Julia for figuring it out."

Molly ran inside, dropped her bag in the hall, and scooped Rosy up. "I missed you, Wigglebutt." Rosy's tail wagged like crazy as she howled and licked Molly's face. "Guess you missed me too, little buddy," Molly giggled.

"Mommy, I missed you last night, but I had the best time with my friends! Can Julia and Emma sleep at our house next time? Maybe you can get us matching pajamas?" "Sounds like a great idea, Molly," her mom hugged her close.

Molly smiled as she reflected, that although three can be tricky sometimes, it is worth it for three times the fun.

A friend for me,
A friend for you

If it's all 3
what will you
do?

Remember to be both
Brave and kind

And three times
the fun

You will
find!

Printed in the USA
CPSIA information can be obtained
at www.ICGtesting.com
JSHW042112240524
63518JS00004B/11